THIS BOOK BELONGS TO:

IF FOUND, REWARD OF _____.

LITTLE BLUE BOOK OF HEARTACHE

Lucy Lovelorn

CIDER MILL
PRESS

BOOK
PUBLISHERS

Kennebunkport, Maine

13-Digit ISBN: 978-1604332704
10-Digit ISBN: 1604332700

This book may be ordered by mail from the publisher.
Please include $2.50 for postage and handling.
Please support your local bookseller first!

Books published by Cider Mill Press Book Publishers are available at special discounts for bulk purchases in the United States by corporations, institutions, and other organizations. For more information, please contact the publisher.

Cider Mill Press Book Publishers
"Where good books are ready for press"
12 Port Farm Road
Kennebunkport, Maine 04046

Visit us on the Web!
www.cidermillpress.com

Design by Alicia Freile, Tango Media
Typography: Bodoni, Futura, Garage Gothic, and Johnny Script
Cover illustration courtesy of Sara M. Lenton
Printed in China

1 2 3 4 5 6 7 8 9 0
First Edition

"If you're going through hell, *keep going.*"

—WINSTON CHURCHILL

"Make the most of what comes and the least of what goes."

—ANONYMOUS

Your heart is pulling itself from your control.

It's sickening. It's lonely. It's unappetizing. Even enraging.

You've broken off from an integral part of your social life, love, and affection.

In simple terms, you're crushed.

Heartbroken.

"The hottest love has the coldest end."

SOCRATES

In all fairness, losing a lover can be excruciating... but it happened.

Eventually, you'll have to put down that pint of ice cream and pick up a new attitude.

The recommended time to do so... is, uh... now.

So put away those tissue boxes and chocolates—unless you want to design your own tissue box online or drink chocolate in shot form, and then I will give you instructions and encourage you. It's time to get over the dude who broke your heart and learn a few things about yourself along the way.

> *"Moving on is simple, it's what you leave behind that makes it so difficult."*
>
> —ANONYMOUS

Perhaps this book stood out to you as a gift or piqued your curiosity.

Perhaps you've reached for reference in these petite pages because you've been torn apart, heart wrenched, love lost, or can't get a grasp on your feelings.

Perhaps, in a pessimistic, gloomy phase, the idea of heartache and heartbreak rang so universal to you that you couldn't possibly imagine how a dainty little blue book could sound the bell much differently... A little blue book of *heartache*?

Fortunately, this book has more than boy bitching and whiney words on how to win him back. Oh no, we will do none of that folding-in sort of deal. This book will help you break out. These pages are for *moving on.*

Now it's in your hands (and doesn't it fit so comfortably and gracefully?), both literally and metaphorically. This book, this *little* book, can help you to make some big moves.

I've been there. Believe me! And I'm passing along tips and quotes to consider, interactive projects to pursue, activities to arouse, and several fill-in-the-blank areas of self-reflection and interaction, making this book a resource as well as a way to release those pent-up feelings… and let them go!

Affectionately,

Lucy Lovelorn

"There is something beautiful about all scars of whatever nature. A scar means the hurt is over, the wound is closed and healed, done with."

—HARRY CREWS

Because heartbreak is a universal theme of human existence, you'll have shoulders to lean on and stories to learn from... and plenty of movies to watch. Movies are wonderful companions.

TOP 5
BREAKUP MOVIES

that Will Let You Wallow in Your Despair

When you just need a good cry, these movies will spur you on. These breakups will make yours feel like a cakewalk. Bust out the tissues and get ready to sob your eyes out.

1. *Out of Africa*
2. *Eternal Sunshine of the Spotless Mind*
3. *Casablanca*
4. *The Way We Were*
5. *Harold & Maude*

Outside-of-the-Box Creativity

Why not create your own tissue box design?
You can even design a tissue box with an ugly
photo of your ex on it to remind you that
you have nothing to cry about.

Make it sensitive and personal, empowering
and elaborate, or a creative collage.

Check out This URL:

http://www.kleenex.com/DesignYourBox.aspx

♥ THE BAD BOY

Breakup offender:

When we dated:

How we broke up:

His most annoying habits:

What worked in this relationship:

What didn't work in this relationship:

What I learned about myself (or what I should do differently):

The best advice:

Given by:

Song that cheered me up the most:

Movie that cheered me up the most:

What I miss most that I left at his place:

TOP 5
BREAKUP MOVIES

to Make You Laugh

Done crying and ready to laugh?
These movies will have you rolling on
the floor with their ridiculous premises
and hilarious breakup scenes.

1. *High Fidelity*

2. *Mallrats*

3. *The Break-Up*

4. *Forgetting Sarah Marshall*

5. *Annie Hall*

"Only time can heal
    your broken heart,
just as only time
can heal his broken
    arms and legs."

—MISS PIGGY

Lean on Me

Now's the time when you need your friends the most, so take full advantage of their availability. Here's a handy place to list friends and family members who will be there for you no matter what. And don't be shy about contacting them—they love and appreciate you and want you to be happy.

Name:

Phone:

Email:

Name:

Phone:

Email:

Name:

Phone:

Email:

Name:

Phone:

Email:

Name:

Phone:

Email:

Name:

Phone:

Email:

Name:

Phone:

Email:

Name:

Phone:

Email:

GIRLS' NIGHT IN

When all you need is a fun night with the girls and little chocolate, this red velvet cake in drink form will have you giggling in no time. Friends, vodka, and laughter—what better to cheer you up with, my dear?

Red Velvet Cocktails

1 part Van Gogh Dutch Chocolate Vodka
1 part Stoli Vanilla Vodka
1 part Chateau Monet Framboise Raspberry Liqueur
Splash of Godiva Chocolate Liqueur

1. Fill a cocktail shaker with ice cubes.
2. Add all ingredients.
3. Shake and strain into a chilled martini glass rimmed with sugar.
4. Cheers!

TOP 10
MOVIES TO WATCH

With Your Girlfriends

Gather your best friends for the ultimate girly movie night with flicks that celebrate strong women and friendship.

1. *Girls Just Wanna Have Fun*
2. *Clueless*
3. *Mean Girls*
4. *Sisterhood of the Traveling Pants*
5. *Thelma & Louise*
6. *Troop Beverly Hills*
7. *Beaches*
8. *A League of Their Own*
9. *Mystic Pizza*
10. *Fried Green Tomatoes*

TOP 10
WORST MOVIES

to Watch After a Breakup

ROMANCE WARNING: While there are plenty of movies that can make you feel better about being newly single, these are not those movies. Do not slip any of these discs into your DVD player. Anything starring Meg Ryan and practically any movie made in the '80s is guaranteed to depress you!

1. *Jerry Maguire*
2. *The Notebook*
3. *Titanic*
4. *Say Anything*
5. *Sleepless in Seattle*
6. *You've Got Mail*
7. *When Harry Met Sally*
8. *Dirty Dancing*
9. *Ghost*
10. *Pretty in Pink*

Natural Woman Cocktail

This all-natural cocktail will make you feel better about being a woman and about being yourself! If you just can't get yourself to the gym to get those endorphins kicking, try one of these instead.

3 parts light rum
1 part cognac
2 splashes lemon juice
2 splashes orgeat almond syrup
(can substitute regular almond syrup)

1. Fill a cocktail shaker with ice cubes.
2. Add all ingredients.
3. Shake and strain into a chilled wine glass filled with ice cubes.
4. Feel like a new woman as you toss it back!

♥ THE PLAYER

Breakup offender:

When we dated:

How we broke up:

His most annoying habits:

What worked in this relationship:

What didn't work in this relationship:

What I learned about myself (or what I should do differently):

The best advice:

Given by:

Song that cheered me up the most:

Movie that cheered me up the most:

He owes me: $

"*I love to shop after a bad relationship. I don't know. I buy a new outfit and it makes me feel better. It just does. Sometimes I see a really great outfit, I'll break up with someone on purpose.*"

—RITA RUDNER

"For my birthday he gave me a coffee table book that clearly demonstrated he had no idea what to get me—after 2 years of dating!—and then dumped me the next day."

—BETH, SILVER SPRING, MD

SEMISWEET REVENGE

If there's a way to eat feelings, there's a right way. Baking! Get nestled in the kitchen, and see how the art of baking can really warm a heart up. Whether you're a natural Betty Crocker or just beginning to find your grind, these recipes will whisk you off into a land of indulgence and tantalizing taste.

Sassy and Single Chocolate Chip Cookies

¾ cup granulated sugar

1 cup packed brown sugar

1 cup butter or margarine, softened

1 egg

2¼ cups all-purpose flour

1 teaspoon baking soda

½ teaspoon salt
1 cup coarsely chopped nuts
1 package (12 ounces) semisweet chocolate chips (2 cups)

1. Heat oven to 375 degrees Fahrenheit.
2. Mix sugars, butter, and egg in large bowl.
   Stir in flour, baking soda, and salt
   (the dough will be stiff). Stir in nuts
   and chocolate chips.
3. Drop dough by rounded tablespoonfuls
   about 2 inches apart onto ungreased
   cookie sheet.
4. Bake 8–10 minutes or until light brown
   (centers will be soft). Cool slightly;
   remove from cookie sheet. Cool on
   wire rack.

Suck-It-Up
Sugar Cookies

½ cup butter

1 cup granulated sugar

2 eggs, well beaten

1 tablespoon milk

1½ cups flour

2 teaspoons baking powder

½ teaspoon salt

1 teaspoon vanilla

¼ cup turbinado sugar (sugar in the raw),
optional

1. Cream butter and sugar.
2. Add eggs and milk, then the flour,
   baking powder and salt.
3. Wrap disk of dough in plastic wrap
   and place in fridge for an hour
   (or up to overnight).
4. Using extra flour to prevent sticking,
   roll out to ¼ to ½ inch thick and cut into
   heart shapes for ironic effect.
5. Sprinkle with turbinado sugar, if desired.
6. Bake at 350 degrees Fahrenheit for
   12–15 minutes.

Write away!

Two magic words, one simple rule: No contact.
The same rule to getting a tattoo applies to lashing
out harshly worded messages: Stop, take a moment
to think about what you may do or say, and decide
if it's really something you'd like for your ex to be
able to forward to anyone he pleases.

But you can write all you want in this little book.

Overthinking? Asking yourself "Why? Why now?
Why me?" Wondering where you went wrong or
wondering where things went south? Have emotions
that you want to express? Here's a place for you
to get it all out of your head on paper. It's amazing
how much better you will feel after writing down
your thoughts, questions, and feelings.

_"You can clutch the past so
tightly to your chest that it
leaves your arms too full to
embrace the present."_

—JAN GLIDEWELL

*"For all sad words of tongue and
pen, the saddest are these,
'It might have been.'"*

—JOHN GREENLEAF WHITTIER

TOP 10
BOOKS

to Guide You Through a Breakup

Having trouble getting past the depression stage? Try picking up one of these books written by professionals. You might find some advice you didn't even know you needed.

1. *There Is Nothing Wrong With You,*
   Cheri Huber

2. *Rebuilding: When Your Relationship Ends,*
   Bruce Fisher

3. *Getting Past Your Breakup,*
   Susan J. Elliott

4. *How to Heal a Broken Heart in 30 Days,*
   Howard Bronson and Mike Riley

5. *Extreme Breakup Recovery,*
   Jeanette Castelli

6. *It's Called a Breakup Because It's Broken*, Greg Behrendt and Amiira Ruotola-Behrendt

7. *How to Survive the Loss of a Love*, Peter McWilliams, Harold Bloomfield, and Melba Colgrove

8. *The Journey from Abandonment to Healing*, Susan Anderson

9. *Don't Call That Man!: A Survival Guide to Letting Go*, Rhonda Findling

10. *How to Fall Out of Love*, Debora Phillips

Once your heart has mended and you're ready to meet someone new, check out:

The Little Pink Book of Dating (Cider Mill Press).

💔 THE LIAR

Breakup offender:

When we dated:

How we broke up:

His most annoying habits:

What worked in this relationship:

What didn't work in this relationship:

What I learned about myself (or what I should do differently):

The best advice:

Given by:

Song that cheered me up the most:

Movie that cheered me up the most:

I hope he...

*Sometimes you just need comfort food.
Like macaroni and cheese. Try this spiced-up
recipe for a cozy night in.*

Spiced
Mac 'n Cheese

1 pound elbow macaroni
2 tablespoons unsalted butter
1 cup heavy cream
1 cup milk
3 tablespoons flour
¼ teaspoon ground mustard powder
Dash of Worcestershire sauce
2 cups sharp cheddar cheese, grated
1 cup Manchego cheese, grated
(can substitute more cheddar or Gruyére,
or Colby)

1 cup Gruyére cheese, grated
(can substitute Swiss or Jarlsberg)
¼ teaspoon cayenne pepper
¼ teaspoon nutmeg
Salt
1 tablespoon salted butter
½ cup breadcrumbs

1. Preheat oven to 350 degrees.
2. Boil some salted water to cook
   the macaroni.
3. Cook the macaroni for about 8 minutes.
   Drain and set aside.
4. In a large pot, melt the unsalted butter
   over medium heat.
5. Heat the milk and cream in a small
   saucepan over medium heat. Set aside.
6. Add the flour to the melted butter and
   stir 1–2 minutes.
7. Add the ground mustard powder and
   Worcestershire sauce and stir.

8. Add the hot milk and cream mixture slowly, whisking constantly to thicken for 3–4 minutes.

9. Mix all the cheeses together and reserve ¾ cup for later.

10. Take remaining cheese and add to pot, alternating with the macaroni, while stirring constantly.

11. Add nutmeg and cayenne pepper and season with salt to taste.

12. Melt salted butter in small skillet.

13. Add breadcrumbs and stir to combine. Cook for about 2 minutes.

14. Grease a 9x13-inch baking pan.

15. Spread macaroni mixture evenly into pan.

16. Top with breadcrumbs and remaining cheese.

17. Bake for 20 minutes at 350 degrees.

Try not to eat the whole pan at once!

"The heart was made to be broken."

—OSCAR WILDE

Brownie Sundae

Need something decadent to take your mind off you-know-who? This combination never fails to make you feel better, even if it can't solve all your problems.

Slice a nice hunk of brownie (whether you start with a brownie mix or just pick up brownies at the market) and put it on a plate. You might want to microwave it for 10–15 seconds to get it nice and fudgy. Then take your favorite brand of vanilla ice-cream and put a big, generous scoop on top. If you're feeling lazy, go ahead and squirt some store-bought chocolate syrup or sauce on top. But if you're feeling fancy, try making this delicious chocolate sauce. It's easy, I promise. And worth it!

Divine Chocolate Sauce

¾ cup heavy cream

1 tablespoon unsalted butter

8 ounces semisweet chocolate chips or chunks

¼ teaspoon pure vanilla extract

1. Mix the cream and butter in a small, heavy saucepan over medium heat.
2. Remove pan from the heat when butter is melted.
3. Place the chocolate and vanilla in a medium heatproof bowl.
4. Add the hot cream mixture and let sit for 2 minutes, then whisk until smooth.
5. Let cool for 5 minutes.

Top your sundae with whipped cream, walnuts, sprinkles, maraschino cherries, or anything else that makes you smile. Enjoy!

♥ THE BRO

Breakup offender:

When we dated:

How we broke up:

His most annoying habits:

What worked in this relationship:

What didn't work in this relationship:

What I learned about myself (or what I should do differently):

The best advice:

Given by:

Song that cheered me up the most:

Movie that cheered me up the most:

The biggest secret I know about him is...

TOP 10
BREAKUP SONGS

for Moving On

Having trouble getting over your ex?
Blast these songs, and you'll be feeling
better in no time.

1. "Cry Me a River," Justin Timberlake

2. "I Will Survive," Gloria Gaynor

3. "Hold On," Wilson Phillips

4. "Song for the Dumped," Ben Folds Five

5. "Smile," Lily Allen

6. "These Boots Are Made for Walking,"
   Nancy Sinatra

7. "You Oughta Know," Alanis Morrisette

8. "You're So Vain," Carly Simon

9. "Don't Go Away Mad (Just Go Away),"
   Motley Crue

10. "The Sign," Ace of Base

"When you break up, *your whole identity* is shattered. *It's like death.*"

—DENNIS QUAID

Rules for Getting Over a Breakup

1. Do not contact your ex, under any circumstances. This will just make it harder to get used to being without him.

2. Think bad thoughts about your ex, especially if that helps you keep rule #1. Don't remember how great things were. Instead, remember the time he forgot your anniversary or was rude to your friends.

3. Give yourself a week to mope, watch bad movies, eat bad food, and drink too much. Then pick yourself up and begin to rebuild.

4. After your week of feeling sorry for yourself, do something positive for yourself or others:

take a class, volunteer, hit the gym, read that book you've been meaning to get to, cook dinner for your roommates—whatever makes you feel good and takes your mind off your ex.

5. *Spend quality time with your friends and family. They will make you feel valued and reaffirm what you already know: You are worthwhile.*

6. *When the time is right, get back out there! It might be a while before you feel like dating again, but sometimes putting yourself out there will help distract you—and you never know who you might meet!*

7. *Stay positive! Consider your ex just a steppingstone on your path to self-improvement, personal growth, and true happiness. Here's to new beginnings!*

Reward Chart

You really ought to get a pat on the back for each day you do NOT contact your ex. Not getting any pats? Well, how about a reward chart to track your progress? Go ahead—use stickers!

WEEK 1

Monday
Tuesday
Wednesday
Thursday
Friday
Saturday
Sunday

WEEK 2

Monday
Tuesday
Wednesday
Thursday
Friday
Saturday
Sunday

CELEBRITY COUPLES

Who Seemed Destined to Be Together Forever… and then Broke Up

Some couples just seem made for each other, at least that's the way they're portrayed in the tabloids. But most celebrity couples don't last, even the ones that appeared to be matches made in heaven. Tom and Nicole? Courtney and David? Donezo. And it all happened in public! Aren't you glad your breakup wasn't broadcast for the world to see? Here are my top 10 couples that seemed too perfect to last…which turned out to be true.

1. Tom Cruise and Nicole Kidman
2. Brad Pitt and Jennifer Aniston
3. Nick Lachey and Jessica Simpson
4. Lance Armstrong and Sheryl Crow
5. Woody Allen and Mia Farrow
6. Paul McCartney and Heather Mills
7. Ben Affleck and Jennifer Lopez
8. Alec Baldwin and Kim Basinger
9. Richie Sambora and Heather Locklear
10. David Arquette and Courtney Cox

"I'm not sure what the future holds but I do know that I'm going to be positive and not wake up feeling desperate. As my dad said, 'Nic, it is what it is, it's not what it should have been, not what it could have been, it is what it is.'"

—NICOLE KIDMAN

💔 THE MAN-CHILD

Breakup offender:

When we dated:

How we broke up:

His most annoying habits:

What worked in this relationship:

What didn't work in this relationship:

What I learned about myself (or what I should do differently):

The best advice:

Given by:

Song that cheered me up the most:

Movie that cheered me up the most:

If bumped into him on the street I would say:

TOP 10
CLASSIC BREAKUP ALBUMS

Broken heart? Crank up these classic breakup albums and commiserate with your buddies who've gone through it too: Bob, Joni, Bruce… they've all been there.

1. *Blood on the Tracks*, Bob Dylan
2. *Blue*, Joni Mitchell
3. *Exile in Guyville*, Liz Phair
4. *Here, My Dear*, Marvin Gaye
5. *Tunnel of Love*, Bruce Springsteen
6. *Pretty Hate Machine*, Nine Inch Nails
7. *Sea Change*, Beck
8. *Rumours*, Fleetwood Mac
9. *Grow Up and Blow Away*, Metric
10. *13*, Blur

He woke up the room was bare
He didn't see her anywhere

He told himself he didn't care
pushed the window open wide

Felt an emptiness inside to
which he just could not relate

Brought on by a simple
twist of fate.

—BOB DYLAN, "SIMPLE TWIST OF FATE"

TOP 5
REASONS

Jerry Broke Up with a Girl
on Seinfeld

In the '90s, *Seinfeld* fans saw Jerry, George, Elaine, and even Kramer go through countless relationships, dates, setups, and, therefore, breakups in true sitcom fasion. Jerry, was king of coming up with inane reasons to dump women. Here are my top 5 reasons Jerry broke up with a girl on *Seinfeld*.

1. In "The Big Salad" episode Jerry can't get over the fact that the woman he's dating once dated his arch-nemesis, Newman. Not only that—Newman dumped her! Jerry can't fathom how that would be possible and obsesses over what must be wrong with her until he can't even look at her without thinking that she wasn't good enough for Newman.

2. In "The Bizarro Jerry" episode, Jerry dates Jillian, but he can't get past the fact that she has "man-hands."

3. After making a pact with George to take relationships more seriously in the episode "The Engagement," Jerry subsequently backs out and breaks up with the woman he's dating because she eats her peas one at a time.

4. In the episode "The Masseuse," Jerry dates a massage therapist who seems to have no problem taking on Kramer as a client but refuses to give Jerry a massage. So he dumps her, obviously.

5. In the episode "The Voice," Jerry and George invent a silly voice that they imagine comes out of the stomach of the woman Jerry is dating. When she finds out about it she leaves him. Later, she offers to get back together with him if he promises to never use the voice again. But he chooses the voice over her.

"There was a big snowstorm so I generously helped my boyfriend dig his car out of the snow. Once it was all done he told me he thought we weren't working out. After all the work I just did!"

—LEIGH, CHERRY HILL, NJ

"Breaking up.
It happens kind of suddenly.
One minute, you're holding hands
walking down the street,
and the next minute,
you're lying on the floor
crying and all the good CDs
are missing."

—KENNEDY KASARES

Chicks' Night Chex Mix

Chex Mix is the perfect, easy treat to munch on while you watch a movie with friends or when you want something savory to spice up your newly single life. Here's an easy recipe that's sure to please.

6 cups Chex cereal (any flavor)
1 cup mini pretzels
1 cup mixed nuts
½ cup butter
¼ teaspoon garlic powder
1 ½ tablespoons Worcestershire sauce
¼ teaspoon salt

1. Preheat oven to 250 degrees.
2. Combine Chex, pretzels, and nuts in a bowl and set aside.
3. Melt butter and mix with remaining ingredients in a large casserole or baking pan.
4. Add dry ingredients and stir to coat.
5. Heat for 1 hour, stirring every 15 minutes.
6. Remove and spread out on paper towels to cool.

"I was never one to patiently pick up broken fragments and glue them together again and tell myself that the mended whole was as good as new. What is broken is broken, and I'd rather remember it as it was at its best than mend it and see the broken pieces as long as I lived."

—MARGARET MITCHELL

"Breaking up is a natural evolution when you try to figure out what you want in life. If you're with an individual who isn't moving in the same direction and at the same rate that you are, it ain't going to work."

—USHER

💔 THE SMARMY NERD

Breakup offender:
....

When we dated:
....

How we broke up:
....
....
....

His most annoying habits:
....
....
....

What worked in this relationship:
....
....
....

What didn't work in this relationship:
....
....
....

What I learned about myself (or what I should do differently):

The best advice:

Given by:

Song that cheered me up the most:

Movie that cheered me up the most:

I've visited his Facebook page _____ times.

Movies have a knack for portraying real life either very well or very poorly. Whether these breakup moments are realistic or not, they certainly nailed the painful and awkward feelings on the head, and managed to get a few laughs in simultaneously.

1. In *Wet Hot American Summer* nice guy Coop (Michael Showalter) finally wins hot girl Katie (Marguerite Moreau), only to be dumped on the last day of camp for the dumb but studly Andy (Paul Rudd). As Katie explains, "I've thought about it and my thing is this: Andy's really hot. And don't get me wrong, you're cute too, but Andy is like, cut from marble."

2. John Cusack was an expert at playing the lovelorn nice guy in the '80s. Perhaps his crowning achievement is during *Say Anything*, when Diane Court (Ione Skye) dumps his character, Lloyd Dobler, in his car and then gives him a pen, following her father's suggestion. This prompts one of the best movie lines ever: "I gave her my heart. She gave me a pen."

3. In *Forgetting Sarah Marshall*, Peter (Jason Segal) is sitting on his couch naked when girlfriend Sarah (Kristin Bell) decides to dump him. Already exposed, he refuses to put on clothes. When Sarah asks him to get dressed, he refuses and asks, "Would you like to pick out the outfit that you break up with me in?"

4. Woody Allen has a definite knack for nailing awkward moments, especially breakups. In *Bananas*, his girlfriend (Louise Lasser) tells him, "There's just something missing for me and I don't know what." Allen spends the rest of the scene trying to find out what it is, discovering that she doesn't find him attractive, he doesn't make her laugh, and she just plain doesn't love him, although none of those are the reasons she wants to dump him.

5. Fred Simmons (Danny McBride) takes immaturity to a new level in *The Foot Fist Way*. When his unsupportive wife challenges him to leave her he accepts, leveling her with this childish insult: "I hope your hair turns into dog [poop] one day." And then he takes off his wedding ring and pees on it.

By the Numbers

(Or, You Are Not Alone in Being Alone)

There are **99.6 million** unmarried Americans over age 18.

—U.S. CENSUS BUREAU, AMERICAN COMMUNITY SURVEY: 2010

39.2% of the unmarried population aged 18 and older were formerly married and **60.8%** have always been single.

—U.S. CENSUS BUREAU'S CURRENT POPULATION SURVEY (CPS), 2008

68% of divorced or widowed Americans plan to remain unmarried.

—GALLUP, 2006

There are more than **31 million** one-person households in the U.S., representing roughly 27% of all households.

—U.S. CENSUS BUREAU, "AMERICA'S FAMILIES AND LIVING ARRANGEMENTS: 2007"

Knitter's Curse

Have you ever made something special or knit someone a scarf, only to be dumped the next week? "Sweater curse" or "curse of the love sweater" are terms used by knitters to illustrate a situation in which a knitter gives a hand-knit sweater or scarf to a significant other, who then breaks up with the knitter soon after. Imagine putting in all that hard work, only to never see your creation again!

In a poll on www.knittersreview.com, they discovered that 41 percent of knitters are careful about knitting for a new love interest, while 30 percent believe the sweater curse is just a superstition. However, 15 percent of knitters surveyed said they had experienced the curse firsthand.

"Love is never lost.
If not reciprocated,
it will flow back and
soften and purify
the heart."

—WASHINGTON IRVING

10 THINGS

to Do After a Breakup

Trying to keep your mind off of Mr. Wrong?
Try one of these ideas that will keep you
busy and make you feel better!

1. Get a mani/pedi. You deserve it!

2. Start a new hobby, or get back into
   an old one.

3. Read that book that's been sitting
   on your shelf forever.

4. Call someone who will be delighted to
   hear from you, like your grandparents.

5. Take a class—cooking, yoga, writing,
   photography… whatever excites you.

6. Bake cookies for your coworkers or
   friends.

7. Organize your old photos that have
   been collecting dust in a shoebox.
   Avoid photos of your ex.

8. Go on a long hike, walk, or bike ride. Enjoy the great outdoors!

9. Go shopping. Don't overspend, but buy yourself something that makes you feel beautiful and special.

10. Volunteer or do some community service in your area. Helping others will make you appreciate what you have—a lot!

"*Alone* also means *available* for someone *outstanding.*"

—GREG BEHRENDT,
*IT'S CALLED A BREAKUP
BECAUSE IT'S BROKEN*

"The tragedy
of love is
indifference."

—AMY LOWELL,
THE TREMBLING OF A LEAF, 1921

♥ THE FRAT BOY

Breakup offender:

When we dated:

How we broke up:

His most annoying habits:

What worked in this relationship:

What didn't work in this relationship:

What I learned about myself (or what I should do differently):

The best advice:

Given by:

Song that cheered me up the most:

Movie that cheered me up the most:

The song/book/movie/TV show that reminds me of him the most is...

"How do you know love is gone? If you said that you would be there at seven and you get there by nine, and he or she has not called the police—it's gone."

—MARLENE DIETRICH

"My friend wooed me into being in a long-distance relationship with him. After months of trying to get him to move to Boston to be with me he decided to break up with me instead. A few months later I found out he *was* moving to Boston… to get back together with the woman he dated before me! Luckily, I found out he was dumped by that same woman a few days after moving. Karma is sweet."

—TIFFANY, BOSTON

TOP 10
BOOKS TO READ

to Put a Smile on Your Face

Reading is a great way to distract yourself, plus you'll learn a lot. These books are light and fun and may even have you giggling out loud.

1. *Love, Loss, and What I Wore*, Ilene Beckerman

2. *What Was I Thinking? 58 Bad Boyfriend Stories*, Barbara Davilman and Liz Dubelman

3. *Bridget Jones's Diary*, Helen Fielding

4. *High Fidelity*, Nick Hornby

5. *The Bedwetter: Stories of Courage, Redemption, and Pee*, Sarah Silverman

6. *Eat, Pray, Love*, Elizabeth Gilbert

7. *Me Talk Pretty One Day*, David Sedaris

8. The Harry Potter series, J.K. Rowling

9. *Simple Times: Crafts for Poor People*, Amy Sedaris

10. *Bossypants*, Tine Fey

"Heaven knows *we need never be* ashamed of our tears, *for they are rain* upon the blinding dust of earth, overlying *our hard hearts.*"

—CHARLES DICKENS

"My desert island, all-time, top-five most memorable breakups, in chronological order, are as follows: Alison Ashmore; Penny Hardwick; Jackie Alden; Charlie Nicholson; and Sarah Kendrew. Those were the ones that really hurt. Can you see your name on that list, Laura? Maybe you'd sneak into the top ten. But there's just no room for you in the top five, sorry. Those places are reserved for the kind of humiliation and heartbreak you're just not capable of delivering."

— ROB GORDON (JOHN CUSACK)
IN *HIGH FIDELITY*

Ross (David Schwimmer): I didn't think there was a relationship to jeopardize. I thought we were broken up.

Rachel (Jennifer Aniston): We were on a break.

Ross: That, for all I knew, could last forever. That, to me, is a breakup.

Rachel: You think you're gonna get out of this on a technicality?

Ross: I'm not trying to "get out" of anything, okay? I thought our relationship was dead.

Rachel: Well, you sure had a hell of a time at the wake.

—*FRIENDS* EPISODE, "THE ONE WHERE ROSS AND RACHEL TAKE A BREAK"

TRY A MARTINI... OR TWO

After a bad breakup sometimes you really need a drink. Or five. But you also want to keep it together and stay classy. That's where the martini comes in. It's got high alcohol content but yet somehow still denotes maturity. Invite a few of the girls over and show them how well you're doing by setting up a classy martini bar. And no girly mixers allowed!

Martini Bar Supplies

Good quality vodka

Good quality gin

Dry vermouth

Olives in brine

Lemon peels

Martini glasses

Cocktail shaker

Ice

The classic martini is simply gin and dry vermouth, but some people prefer vodka instead of gin. And of course, you can garnish it with an olive or lemon peel, or if you like it "dirty," add in some brine from the olives. Here's a simple recipe.

Basic Martini Recipe

1¾ ounces gin or vodka
¾ ounce vermouth
Olives, lemon peel, or olive brine

1. Fill a cocktail shaker with ice.
2. Pour gin or vodka and vermouth into a cocktail shaker. If you are having it dirty, add a ½ ounce of olive brine.
3. Stir or shake mixture.
4. Strain into martini glass.
5. Garnish with olives or lemon peel.
6. Sip slowly and responsibly.

Ex-Or-Size

Why not put all your pent up pain into a killer workout routine? Exercising will not only help you lose weight and tone your muscles so you will look amazing, it also releases endorphins, which will make you feel happy and satisfied. Sweat out your stress and feel good about yourself in the process! Instead of moping around and eating that chocolate cake, head to the gym and try doing 30 minutes of cardio and 30 minutes of muscle toning three times a week. If you have time, try to go to a yoga or Pilates class once a week, too. You'll be amazed at how good you feel—and look. Oh, and so will your ex.

"Nothing takes the taste out of peanut butter quite like unrequited love."

—CHARLIE BROWN

Meditate Your Pain Away

Meditation can be a powerful tool to help you get over your grief. It's calming, rejuvenating, restorative, and can help with increased self-awareness. Meditating will allow you to set aside some important "me" time and to realize your self-worth. Here's a quick and easy meditation guide, but if you're serious you should take some books out of the library or poke around on the Internet for more guidance.

1. *Sit down in a quiet place, free from distractions. If you'd like to have music playing, choose something soothing and calm.*

2. *Sit in a chair or on the floor with your spine as straight as possible and close your eyes.*

3. *Inhale deeply, allowing your rib cage to expand.*

4. *Exhale slowly and become aware of each breath you take.*

5. *As you continue breathing, allow thoughts to enter and exit your mind freely, but always refocus on your breathing.*

"Pain is inevitable.
Suffering is optional."

—ZEN APHORISM

Pain may be inevitable, but why should you be the only one to suffer? Why not make a paper voodoo doll of your ex (all in jest, of course).

♥ THE JOCK

Breakup offender:

When we dated:

How we broke up:

His most annoying habits:

What worked in this relationship:

What didn't work in this relationship:

What I learned about myself (or what I should do differently):

The best advice:

Given by:

Song that cheered me up the most:

Movie that cheered me up the most:

If I decided to take revenge on him, here's what I would do:

Don't speak

I know just what you're saying
So please stop explaining
Don't tell me cause it hurts

Don't speak

I know what you're thinking
I don't need your reasons
Don't tell me cause it hurts.

—"DON'T SPEAK," NO DOUBT

Are you lonesome tonight,
Do you miss me tonight?

Are you sorry we
drifted apart?

Does your memory stray to
a brighter sunny day

When I kissed you and called
you sweetheart?

—"ARE YOU LONESOME TONIGHT?"
ELVIS PRESLEY

"The only thing worse than a smug married couple; lots of smug married couples."

—BRIDGET JONES'S DIARY

"A woman *without a man,* is like a fish *without a bicycle.*"

—GLORIA STEINEM

Cheer Up Chili

*Sometimes you just need something to eat
that feels like home and warms your insides.
Chili is a wonderful and easy dish that will
make enough to have leftovers for several days.
Plus, it smells delicious as it cooks!*

1 tablespoon vegetable oil
½ cup chopped onion
½ cup chopped green or red bell pepper
1 ½ pounds lean ground beef
2 teaspoons chopped jalapeno pepper
2 ½ tablespoons chili powder
½ teaspoon ground cumin
Salt and pepper to taste
½ cup water
1 28-ounce can diced tomatoes,
undrained
1 15-ounce can kidney beans,
undrained

1. Add oil to a large pot over medium heat.
2. Add onions and peppers and sauté for about 5 minutes.
3. Add ground beef and cook for another 5 minutes, until beef is browned.
4. Add remaining ingredients except beans and stir.
5. Bring to a boil and then reduce heat to low.
6. Let simmer for 1½ hours.
7. Add beans and stir. Cook until beans are heated through.
8. Serve with sour cream it desired.

"I am a marvelous housekeeper. Every time I leave a man I keep his house."

—ZSA ZSA GABOR

"Happiness *is the china shop;* love is the bull."

—H. L. MENCKEN

Get It Out!

Are breakup worries still circling in your head?
Get them out on paper.

Valentino, I don't think so.

*You watching MTV while I lie
dreaming in an empty bed*

And come to think of it

I was misled

My flat, my food, my everything

And thoughts inside my head

—"I NEVER LOVED YOU ANYWAY,"
THE CORRS

"Life is so brief that we should not glance either too far backwards or forward... therefore study how to fix our happiness in our glass and in our plate."

—GRIMOD DE LA REYNIÈRE

Sweet Revenge

While revenge is probably not the ideal way to get over an ex, it may make you feel better for a little while. But don't do anything illegal! It's not worth the possibility of jail time, trust me!

Sex-Out: Promise your ex mind-blowing breakup sex, then leave him in the cold. You can either not show up, or meet him, ask him to get naked, cuff him to the bed, and then leave. But make sure you're strong enough to actually walk away before doing the deed! (Hmm… is this illegal?)

Tell All: Tell all his dirty little secrets on a blog—you know, the ones about his worst fears, how bad he is in bed, and the awful things he said about his friends and family. WARNING: Remember that things spread fast on the Internet and there's nothing to stop your ex from releasing all of *your* dirty little secrets, too!

Make His Stuff Work For You: Take anything your ex left behind in your pad and anything he ever gave you as a gift and put it up on eBay. Send your ex the link so he can see just how much money you're making off him.

Be All You Can Be: The best revenge really is moving on and being fabulous. Get in shape, spend time on your hobbies, and just enjoy life. The next time you bump into your ex he will be stunned at how happy and put-together you are, and of course at how great you look!

"He said, 'You know, I'm just waiting for lightning to strike me and feel love at first sight.' I said, 'I'm waiting for lightening to strike you, too.'"

—SHANNA, BROOKLYN, NY

"Have you ever been in love?
Horrible isn't it?
It makes you so vulnerable.
*It opens your chest
and it opens up your heart*
and it means that
someone can get inside you
and mess you up."

—NEIL GAIMAN

♥ THE CHEATER

Breakup offender:

When we dated:

How we broke up:

His most annoying habits:

What worked in this relationship:

What didn't work in this relationship:

What I learned about myself (or what I should do differently):

The best advice:

Given by:

Song that cheered me up the most:

Movie that cheered me up the most:

I knew he was cheating when...

"*Ah, yes, 'divorce,'
from the Latin word
meaning to rip out
a man's genitals
through his wallet.*"

—ROBIN WILLIAMS

"One reason
people get divorced
is that they run out
of gift ideas."

—ROBERT BYRNE

ANNOYING HABITS CHECKLIST

Check off each of these bad habits that any of your exes practiced. And of course, we already know you don't have any annoying habits, right?

- [ ] Smoked cigarettes
- [ ] Farted too much
- [ ] Burped too much
- [ ] Cut his nails in inappropriate places
- [ ] Didn't call when he said he would
- [ ] Texted instead of calling
- [ ] Watched TV when you're trying to have a conversation
- [ ] Didn't put the toilet seat down
- [ ] Spit
- [ ] Scratched his family jewels all the time
- [ ] Picked his wedgies constantly
- [ ] Gawked at other women

☐ Left dirty clothes everywhere except the hamper

☐ Didn't clean the sink after shaving

☐ Picked his nose

☐ Refused to get new underwear even though his were full of holes

☐ Constantly played video games

☐ Bothered you about how much money you spent shopping

☐ Never wanted to spend time with your friends or family

☐ Left dirty dishes in the sink

☐ Had bad breath

☐ Always had food stuck in his teeth

☐ Didn't perform foreplay enough

☐ Always wanted to split the bill

Don't you feel better now?

PERKS TO BEING SINGLE

Save yourself from emotional torture, and your friends from tortured ears. Before your next breakup, remind yourself of the benefits of being single. I'll get you started with some ideas:

- Less laundry.
- Worry-free bad hair days and makeup-free mornings.
- You can travel to an exotic place and have no strings attached—eye candy galore—and potential to learn a whole new language of love.

"When one door closes, another opens; but we often look so long and so regretfully upon the closed door that we do not see the one which has opened for us."

—ALEXANDER GRAHAM BELL

"You know it's love when all you want is that person to be happy, even if you're not part of their happiness."

—JULIA ROBERTS

ABOUT CIDER MILL PRESS
BOOK PUBLISHERS

Good ideas ripen with time. From seed to harvest,
Cider Mill Press brings fine reading, information,
and entertainment together between the covers of
its creatively crafted books. Our Cider Mill bears
fruit twice a year, publishing a new crop
of titles each spring and fall.

*Where Good Books Are
Ready for Press*

Visit us on the web at
www.cidermillpress.com
or write to us at
12 Port Farm Road
Kennebunkport, Maine 04046

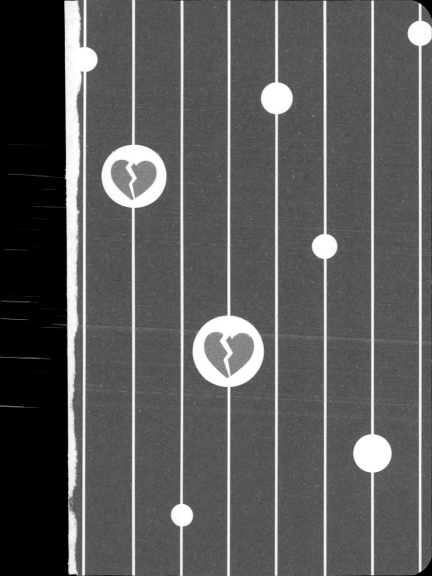